Books by W. S. Merwin

THE VIXEN

THE VIXEN

POEMS BY

W S. MERWIN

ALFRED A. KNOPF NEW YORK

1996

SOME OF THESE POEMS WERE ORIGINALLY PUBLISHED IN THE FOLLOWING PERIODICALS:

ANTAEUS: *Possessions*

THE ATLANTIC MONTHLY: *End of a Day, Other Time, Vehicles, The Speed of Light, Green Fields*

BOULEVARD: *Bodies of Water*

THE COLORADO REVIEW: *Authority, Walkers, Thread, Upland House, A Taste*

DIA CENTER FOR THE ARTS: *Gate*

FIELD: *Old Question, One Time*

GRAND STREET: *After Fires, Cisterns*

THE HUDSON REVIEW: *Garden*

THE NATION: *In the Doorway, Battues, The Red*

THE NEW YORK REVIEW OF BOOKS: *Ancestral Voices, One of the Lives*

THE NEW YORK TIMES: *Threshold*

THE NEW YORKER: *The West Window, Net, Letters, Present, Romanesque, Dry Ground, Snake, Season, Emergence, Peire Vidal, Old Walls, The Furrow, Legacies, Substance, Passing, Vixen, A Given Day*

THE PARIS REVIEW: *Hölderlin at the River, Night Singing*

PARTISAN REVIEW: *Commemoratives, White Morning, Forgotten Streams*

POETRY: *Fox Sleep, Oak Time, Color Merchants, Entry, Passing, The Bird, Returning Season, Untouched, The View, The Shortest Night, Old Sound, Distant Morning, Traces, The Time Before, Portrait, Completion*

POETRY NORTHWEST: *Ill Wind, François de Maynard 1582–1646*

VUELTA: *Old Question*

WILDERNESS: *Late*

Library of Congress Cataloging-in-Publication Data
Merwin, W. S. (William Stanley), 1927–
 The vixen : poems / by W. S. Merwin.—1st ed.
  p. cm.
 ISBN 0–679–44477–7
 I. Title.
PS3563.E75V58   1996   95–30283
811'.54—dc20   CIP

For Harry Ford

Contents

Contents

THE VIXEN

FOX SLEEP

On a road through the mountains with a friend many years ago
    I came to a curve on a slope where a clear stream
flowed down flashing across dark rocks through its own
    echoes that could neither be caught nor forgotten
it was the turning of autumn and already
    the mornings were cold with ragged clouds in the hollows
long after sunrise but the pasture sagging like a roof
    the glassy water and flickering yellow leaves
in the few poplars and knotted plum trees were held up
    in a handful of sunlight that made the slates on the silent
mill by the stream glisten white above their ruin
    and a few relics of the life before had been arranged
in front of the open mill house to wait
    pale in the daylight out on the open mountain
after whatever they had been made for was over
    the dew was drying on them and there were few who took that road
who might buy one of them and take it away somewhere
    to be unusual to be the only one
to become unknown a wooden bed stood there on rocks
    a cradle the color of dust a cracked oil jar iron pots
wooden wheels iron wheels stone wheels the tall box of a clock
    and among them a ring of white stone the size of an
embrace set into another of the same size
    an iron spike rising from the ring where the wooden
handle had fitted that turned it in its days as a hand mill
    you could see if you looked closely that the top ring
that turned in the other had been carved long before in the form
    of a fox lying nose in tail seeming to be
asleep the features worn almost away where it
    had gone around and around grinding grain and salt
to go into the dark and to go on and remember

    *   *   *

What I thought I had left I kept finding again
    but when I went looking for what I thought I remembered
as anyone could have foretold it was not there
    when I went away looking for what I had to do
I found that I was living where I was a stranger
    but when I retraced my steps the familiar vision

Fox Sleep

turned opaque and all surface and in the wrong places
    and the places where I had been a stranger appeared to me
to be where I had been at home called by name and answering
    getting ready to go away and going away

        *   *   *

Every time they assembled and he spoke to them
    about waking there was an old man who stood listening
and left before the others until one day the old man stayed
    and Who are you he asked the old man
and the old man answered I am not a man
    many lives ago I stood where you are standing
and they assembled in front of me and I spoke to them
    about waking until one day one of them asked me
When someone has wakened to what is really there
    is that person free of the chain of consequences
and I answered yes and with that I turned into a fox
    and I have been a fox for five hundred lives
and now I have come to ask you to say what will
    free me from the body of a fox please tell me
when someone has wakened to what is really there
    is that person free of the chain of consequences
and this time the answer was That person sees it as it is
    then the old man said Thank you for waking me
you have set me free of the body of the fox
    which you will find on the other side of the mountain
I ask you to bury it please as one of your own
    that evening he announced a funeral service
for one of them but they said nobody has died
    then he led them to the other side of the mountain
and a cave where they found a fox's body
    and he told them the story and they buried the fox
as one of them but later one of them asked
    what if he had given the right answer every time

        *   *   *

Once again I was there and once again I was leaving
    and again it seemed as though nothing had changed

4

even while it was all changing but this time
    was a time of ending this time the long marriage was over
the orbits were flying apart it was autumn again
    sunlight tawny in the fields where the shadows
each day grew longer and the still afternoons
    ripened the distance until the sun went down
across the valley and the full moon rose out of the trees
    it was the time of year when I was born and that evening
I went to see friends for the last time and I came back
    after midnight along the road white with the moon
I was crossing the bars of shadow and seeing ahead of me
    the wide silent valley full of silver light
and there just at the corner of the land that I had
    come back to so many times and now was leaving
at the foot of the wall built of pale stone I saw the body
    stretched in the grass and it was a fox a vixen
just dead with no sign of how it had come to happen
    no blood the long fur warm in the dewy grass
nothing broken or lost or torn or unfinished
    I carried her home to bury her in the garden
in the morning of the clear autumn that she had left
    and to stand afterward in the turning daylight

      *   *   *

There are the yellow beads of the stonecrops and the twisted flags
    of dried irises knuckled into the hollows
of moss and rubbly limestone on the waves of the low wall
    the ivy has climbed along them where the weasel ran
the light has kindled to gold the late leaves of the cherry tree
    over the lane by the house chimney there is the roof
and the window looking out over the garden
    summer and winter there is the field below the house
there is the broad valley far below them all with the curves
    of the river a strand of sky threaded through it
and the notes of bells rising out of it faint as smoke
    and there beyond the valley above the rim of the wall
the line of mountains I recognize like a line of writing
    that has come back when I had thought it was forgotten

OAK TIME

Storms in absence like the ages before I was anywhere
    and out in the shred of forest through the seasons
a few oaks have fallen towering ancients elders
    the last of elders standing there while the wars drained away
they slow-danced with the ice when time had not discovered them
    in a scrap of what had been their seamless fabric these late ones
are lying shrouded already in eglantine and brambles
    bird-cherry nettles and the tangled ivy
that prophesies disappearance and had already
    crept into the shadows they made when they held up their lives
where the nightingales sang even in the daytime
    and cowbells echoed through the long twilight of summer
the ivy knew the way oh the knowing ivy
    that was never wrong how few now the birds seem to be
no animals are led out any longer from the barns
    after the milking to spend the night pastured here
they are all gone from the village Edouard is gone
    who walked out before them to the end of his days
keeping an eye on the walnuts still green along the road
    when the owl watched from these oaks and in the night
I would hear the fox that barked here bark and be gone

GATE

Once I came back to the leaves just as they were falling
    into the rattling of magpies and the waving flights
through treetops beyond the long field tawny with stubble
    a scatter of sheep wandered there circling slowly
as a galaxy ferrying the gray lights that were theirs
    wading into their shadows with the stalks whispering
under them and the day shining out of the straw
    all the way to the break in the wall where the lane goes down
into old trees to turn at the end and follow
    the side of the cliff and I stopped there to look as always
out over the hedgerows and the pastures lying
    face upward filled with the radiance before sunset
one below the other down to the haze along the river
    each of them broader than I had remembered them
like skies with sheep running molten in the lanes between them
    clonking of sheep bells drifting up through the distance
I watched the shadow climbing the fields and I turned
    uphill to come to the top gate and the last barn
the sun still in the day and my shadow going on
    out into the upland and I saw they were milking
it was that hour and it seemed all my friends were there
    we greeted each other and we walked back out to the gate
talking and saw the last light and our shadows gesturing
    far out along the ridge until the darkness gathered them
and we went on standing here believing there were other words
    we stood here talking about our lives in the autumn

THRESHOLD

Swallows streaking in and out through the row of broken
     panes over the front door went on with their conversation
of afterthoughts whatever they had been settling
     about early summer and nests and the late daylight
and the vacant dwellings of swallows in the beams
     let their dust filter down as I brought in my bed
while the door stood open onto the stone sill smoothed to water
     by the feet of inhabitants never known to me
and when I turned to look back I did not recognize a thing
     the sound of flying whirred past me a voice called far away
the swallows grew still and bats came out light as breath
     around the stranger by himself in the echoes
what did I have to do with anything I could remember
     all I did not know went on beginning around me
I had thought it would come later but it had been waiting

THE WEST WINDOW

When the cracked plaster and patchwork of thin bricks
    and dry boards that were partitions out of lives not long gone
had fallen and the room emerged empty and entire
    I was seeing something that had been there in the house
through births ages deaths but that no one had set eyes on
    a whole that the rooms had been part of all the time
then the wordless light fingered the rubble on the floor
    as though it had known it by touch at another time
and the windows went on with their lives as though they were
    separate and stood outside where each had a sky of its own
to the south the wrecked doorway toward the slope and the village
    to the north the opening onto fields and valley
 but it was the west window that the moment seemed to be
    coming from while the day moved in silence through the tall
casements and ivy and it held up in the hewn edges
    of its stone frame the stairs winding under the rock face
below the lane and garden wall and the pigeons on a gable roof
    how completely all of it knew itself even to the dust at my feet
and the dark holes in the floor the shards of plaster
    they had been there before and would remain in their own time
as they appeared to me in the light from that window

AUTHORITY

At the beginning the oldest man sat on the corner
    of the garden wall by the road under a vast
walnut tree known to have been there always
    he came back in the afternoon to the cave of shade
in his broad black hat black jacket the striped gray
    wool trousers once worn only to church in winter
with a cane on either side resting against the stones
    he said when your legs have gone all you can do
is to sit this way and be useless I believe God
    has forgotten me but I think and I remember
he said that is what I am doing I am thinking
    and things come to me now when nobody else knows them
he was visited by the dazzling of accidents the boy
    who caught his hand in the trip hammer and it came out
like cigarette paper the man with both crushed legs
    dangling and the woman murdered and his father the blacksmith
forging the iron fence to put around the place
    out on the bare slope where she had fallen I could never
be the smith my father was as he always told me
    I was good enough you know but I never had
the taste needed for scythe blades sickles kitchen knives
    we preferred to use carriage springs to make them from
in the forge outside the barn there and his were sought after
    oh when he had sold all he took to the fair the others
could begin I still have the die for stamping the name
    of the village in the blade at the end so you could be sure

WALKERS

Then I could walk for a whole day over the stony
    ridges along fallen walls and lanes matted with
sloe branches and on through oak woods and around springs
    low cliffs mouths of caves and out onto open
hillsides overlooking valleys adrift in the distance
    and after the last sheep in their crumbling pastures
fenced with cut brush there would be only the burr of a wren
    scolding from rocks or one warbler's phrase repeated
following through the calls of crows and the mossed hush
    of ruins palmed in the folds of the crumpled slopes
in deep shade with the secret places of badgers
    and no other sound it was the edge of a silence
about to become as though it had never been
    for a while before emerging again unbroken
once I looked up a bank straight into the small eyes
    of a boar watching me and we stared at each other
in that silence before he turned and went on with his
    walk and once when I had dried figs in my pocket
I met an old woman who laughed and said this was the way
    she had come all her life and between two fingers she
accepted a fig saying Oh you bring me dainties
    there was still the man always astray in the dark suit
and string tie who might emerge from a barn and gaze
    skyward saying Ah Ah something had happened to him
in the war they said but he never took anything
    and there was the gnarled woman from a remote hamlet
hurrying head down never looking at anyone
    to a house she owned that had stood empty for decades
there to dust the tables sweep out the rooms cut weeds
    in the garden set them smouldering and as quickly
bolt the windows lock the door and be on her way

ILL WIND

As long as the south wind keeps thrashing the green branches
　　　　caught in themselves so that they twist trying to find somewhere
else to be left in peace while the wind-scorched leaves wither
　　　　curl and are snatched away whipped in the hissing rush
over restless litter and cracked ground until the boughs
　　　　groan crash finally snap striking back flailing
finding as they fall the vain gestures of feelings
　　　　never to be known and thick trunks split and the tender
seedlings lie down and shrivel and we sleep lightly
　　　　as dust to be wakened by wind wearing at us
from inside all through the gray dark and into
　　　　the bleached morning attaching itself to us
dragging us keeping at us weighing upon us
　　　　like rumors of dreaded news sapping us wherever
we turn until we suspect it of having a mind
　　　　devious implacable malevolent that we
cannot but recognize while denying it we are sharing
　　　　that apprehension with ancestors many as leaves
this was the scourge of harvests that devastated
　　　　vineyards sent roofs sailing brought down the big trees
those who have watched over the lives of things have known it
　　　　wherever they were and reminded themselves that always
it went as it came and the fragile green survived it

NET

We were sitting along the river as the daylight
    faded in high summer too slowly to be followed
a pink haze gathering beyond the tall poplars
    over on the island and late swallows snapping at gnats
from the glassy reaches above the shallows
    where feathers of a gray mist were appearing
trout leapt like the slapping of hands behind the low voices
    that went on talking of money with the sound of rapids
running through them the boots smelled of former water
    the piled nets smelled of the deaths of fish I will know now
how night comes with eyes of its own to a river
    and then it was dark and we were seeing by river light
as the oldest got up first taking a coil of rope
    down and disappeared into the sound then we
went after him one by one stepping into the cold pull
    of the current to feel the round stones slip farther
below us and we uncoiled the nets with the voices
    scarcely reaching us over the starlit surface
until we stood each alone hearing only the river
    and held the net while the unseen fish brushed past us

GARDEN

When I still had to reach up for the door knob
    I was wondering why the Lord God whoever that was
who had made everything in heaven and the earth
    and knew it was good and that nobody could hurt it
had decided to plant a garden apart
    from everything and put some things inside it
leaving all the rest outside where we were
    so the garden would be somewhere we would never see
and we would know of it only that it could not be known
    a bulb waiting in pebbles in a glass of water
in sunlight at a window You will not be wanting
    the garden too the husband said as an afterthought
but I said yes I would which was all I knew of it
    even the word sounding strange to me for the seedy
tatter trailing out of its gray ravelled walls
    on the ridge where the plateau dropped away to the valley
old trees shaded the side toward the village
    lichens silvered the tangled plum branches hiding
the far end the scrape of the heavy door as it dragged
    across the stone sill had deepened its indelible
groove before I knew it and a patch of wilting
    stalks out in the heat shimmer stood above potatoes
someone had cultivated there among the stately nettles
    it was not time yet for me to glimpse the clay
itself dark in rain rusting in summer shallow
    over fissured limestone here and there almost
at the surface I had yet to be shown how the cold
    softened it what the moles made of it where the snake
smiled on it from the foot of the wall what the redstart
    watched in it what would prosper in it what it would become
I had yet to know how it would appear to me

LETTERS

You could not see the valley unrolled below me
    the rusted towers haunting one hill and the glint
of farms on a faded south slope across the suspended
    still afternoon unrepeatable as a cloud
that I watched while I wrote to you taking up at a point
    farther along it the edge of that loose fabric
already of some length but by then torn here and there
    frayed worn stained its pattern always complicated
but beginning to emerge perhaps as what we could
    recognize after all under the name of friendship
and from what gulfs and distances and how fitfully
    from there on it came to remind us of the time
when you had always made much of being my
    elder and then you confessed your amazement at finding
yourself past forty with all the early ambitions
    surfeited all that brilliance rewarded you were no longer
boasting but finding it empty wondering what
    else there might be where else to look and you raised
the subject of the fleet in the bay at Aulis
    on the way to Troy when the wind dropped we would return
to that through the years almost as often as you
    went over your classic animosities
dissolving marriage continuing restlessness
    yet in your words so little appeared in color
of the countenance of your life you wrote from England
    alluding to pastoral scenery as though it
belonged to you but you complained of the English evening
    always about to descend so that I thought I could see that
but even in your late desperate grasping
    at a youthfulness that had never been yours
in your confidences I could not see her there were only
    your spiralling explanations your insistence
your vertigo it was spring then and the stove burning low
    smelled of tar while honeysuckle swayed at the window
and along the rough wall quince petals were holding up
    the light that was theirs as it was passing through them
among the many things of which we would not have spoken

COMMEMORATIVES

This was the day when the guns fell silent one time
  on old calendars before I was born then the bells
clanged to say it was over forever again
  and again as they would every year when the same
hour had found the yellow light in the poplars
  tan leaves of sycamores drifting across the square
out of the world and those who remembered the day
  it was first over sat around tables holding
reflections in their hands thinking here we are
  while the speeches reverberated in their faces
here we are we lived these are our faces now we are singing
  these are ourselves standing out under the same trees
smoking talking of money we are the same we lived
  with our moustaches our broadening features our swellings
at the belt our eyes from our time and in that chill air
  of November with its taste of bronze I took the winding
road up the mountain until it hissed in the chestnut forest
  where once the hunters had followed the edge of the ice
I came to sounds of a stream crossing stones a hare moving like
  one of the shadows jays warning through bare branches
the afternoon was drawing toward winter the signposts
  at the crossroads even then were rusted over

WHITE MORNING

On nights toward the end of summer an age of mist
    has gathered in the oaks the box thickets the straggling
eglantines it has moved like a hand unable to believe
    the face it touches over the velvet of wild thyme
and the vetches sinking with the weight of dew it has found
    its way without sight into the hoofprints of cows
the dark nests long empty the bark hanging alone the narrow
    halls among stones and has held it all in a cloud
unseen the whole night as in a mind where I came
    when it was turning white and I was holding a thin
wet branch wrapped in lichens because all I had thought
    I knew had to be passed from branch to branch through the empty
sky and whatever I reached then and could recognize
    moved toward me out of the cloud and was still the sky
where I went on looking until I was standing on
    the wide wall along the lane to the hazel grove
where we went one day to cut handles that would last
    the crows were calling around me to white air
I could hear their wings dripping and hear small birds with lights
    breaking in their tongues the cold soaked through me I was able
after that morning to believe stories that once
    would have been closed to me I saw a carriage go under
the oaks there in full day and vanish I watched animals there
    I sat with friends in the shade they have all disappeared
most of the stories have to do with vanishing

COLOR MERCHANTS

They had no color themselves nothing about them
    suggested the spectrum from which they were making
a living the one who had arrived with experience
    from the city to open a shop in the old square
wearing his glasses on his forehead vowing allegiance
    to rusticity understanding what anyone
wanted to the exact tone a head waiter of hues
    or the one who had gone away to be a painter
in Paris and had come back in the war no longer
    young wearing his beret with a difference
a hushed man translucent as paper who displayed
    artists' supplies in a town without artists and could
recall the day when he and a few old men
    and farm boys ambushed the column of Germans heading
north to the channel after the invasion
    and held them up for most of an hour and afterward
how he had sat with his easel day after day at one end
    of the low bridge where the guns had blackened that
summer afternoon and had listened to the rustle
    of the leaves of limes and plane trees and to the shallow
river whispering one syllable on the way
    to the island and he had tried to find the right shades
for the empty street and the glare on the running water

ENTRY

When it seems that the world is made of a single
    summer as it always has been and that the gray leaves
will hang that same way without moving above the empty
    road until the end while the wheat goes on standing
in its sleep with no dreams soundless and shining into
    the hovering day along the stopped film of the river
and when the doors facing south have turned to stone every one
    and the parched syllable of cicadas through the hush
of fields hangs still in the light and from shuttered
    windows voices sift like the settling of dust
all at once the blank sky will be half dark with the black
    cloud welling out of which a cold wind rolls and the first
thunder splits all around to build upon its own
    deafening echoes then suddenly the light will be only
the weight of rain cascading shot through with lightning
    at that time if you are away from home and can stumble
to any house they will let you in to a dark room
    that will close behind you at the heart of the roar
and you will see as through water an unknown face but you
    will hear no sound it makes and behind it others
will be looking up in silence from around a table
    knowing nothing about you except why you are there

FORGOTTEN STREAMS

The names of unimportant streams have fallen
    into oblivion the syllables have washed away
but the streams that never went by name never raised the question
    whether what has been told and forgotten is in
another part of oblivion from what was never remembered
    no one any longer recalls the Vaurs and the Divat
the stream Siou Sujou Suzou and every speaker
    for whom those were the names they have all become
the stream of Lherm we do not speak the same language
    from one generation to another and we
can tell little of places where we ourselves have lived
    the whole of our lives and still less of neighborhoods
where our parents were young or the parents of our friends
    how can we say what the sound of voices was or what
a skin felt like or a mouth everything that the mouths did
    and the tongues the look of the eyes the animals the fur
the unimportant breath not far from here an unknown
    mason dug up a sword five hundred years old
the only thing that is certain about it now
    is that in the present it is devoured with rust
something keeps going on without looking back

PRESENT

She informed me that she had a tree of mirabelles
    told me it was the only one anywhere around
she did not want everyone to realize she had it
    it might go for years and bear nothing at all
flowering with the other plums but then nothing
    and another year it would be covered with mirabelles
you know they are not so big as all the others
    but they are more delicate for those acquainted with them
she promised me mirabelles if it was the year for them
    she lived in a house so small she must have been able
to reach anything from where she was and her garden
    was scarcely larger she grew corn salad in winter
after Brussels sprouts well it was a cold garden
    facing north so it was slow in spring better for summer
one of the knotted gray trees leaning against the wall
    to the south was the mirabelle a snow of plum blossoms
swept across the valley in the morning sunlight
    of a day in March and moved up the slope hour by hour
she told me later she thought it would be a year
    of mirabelles unless it froze when she bent in her garden
she disappeared in the rows it took her a long time
    to stand up to turn around to let herself through
the gate to walk to do anything at my age
    I have all I need she said if I keep warm
late one day that summer she appeared at the wall
    carrying a brown paper bag wet at the bottom
the mirabelles she whispered but she would not come in
    we sat on the wall and opened the bag look she said
how you can see through them and each of us held up
    a small golden plum filled with the summer evening

PASSING

The morning after the house almost burned down
    one night at the end of a season of old wood
of dust and tunnels in beams and of renewals and the tuning
    of hinges and putty soft around new panes in the clear
light of autumn and then the fire had led itself
    in the dark through the fragrance of doors and ceilings
the last flame was scarcely out in the cellar
    and we were still splashing soaked sooty red-eyed
in black puddles all the neighbors with vineyard sprayers
    hosing into cracks and the acrid steam persisting
in our breath when the message came from the village
    the telephone it was my father on his
impromptu journey asking me to be surprised
    not taking in a word about the fire but inquiring
about changing money about where I could meet him
    about trains for the Holy Land and when I drove him
from the station the long way round so he could see the country
    for the first time he seemed to be seeing nothing
and I did not know that it was the only time

THE BIRD

Might it be like this then to come back descending
  through the gray sheeted hour when it is said that dreams
are to be believed the moment when the ghosts go home
  with the last stars still on far below in a silence
that deepens like water a sinking softly toward them
  to find a once-familiar capital half dissolved
like a winter its faces piled in their own wreckage
  and over them unfinished towers of empty
mirrors risen framed in air then beside pewter rivers
  under black nests in the naked poplars arriving
at the first hesitations of spring the thin leaves
  shivering and the lights in them and at cold April with trees
all in white its mullein wool opening on thawed banks
  cowslips and mustard in the morning russet cows on green slopes
running clouds behind hands of willows the song of the wren
  and both recognizing and being recognized with doubting
belief neither stranger nor true inhabitant
  neither knowing nor not knowing coming at last
to the door in sunlight and seeing as through glasses far
  away the old claims the longings to stay and to leave
the new heights of the trees the children grown tall and polite
  the animal absences and scarcely touching anything
holding it after all as uncertainly
  as the white blossoms were held that have been blown down
most of them in one night or this empty half
  of a bird's egg flung out of the bare flailing branches

RETURNING SEASON

When the spring sun finds the village now it is empty
    but from the beginning this was the afterlife
it was not so apparent a generation gone
    these were still roofs under which the names were born
that came home winter evenings before all the wars to sleep
    through freezing nights when the dogs curled low in the cow barns
and sheep nudged their rank clouds in the dark as one
    now only wagons sleep there and stalled plows
and machine skeletons rusting around stopped notes
    of far-off bells in a cold longer than winter's
they will not be wanted again nor wake into any life
    when the recesses from a better world begin
the year goes on turning and the barns remain without breath
    and now after sundown a city bulb keeps an eye on the village
until past midnight but the owls sweep by the low eaves
    and over black gardens in the light of finished stars

END OF A DAY

In the long evening of April through the cool light
    Baille's two sheep dogs sail down the lane like magpies
for the flock a moment before he appears near the oaks
    a stub of a man rolling as he approaches
smiling and smiling and his dogs are afraid of him
    we stand among the radiant stones looking out across
green lucent wheat and earth combed red under bare walnut limbs
    bees hanging late in cowslips and lingering bird cherry
stumps and brush that had been the grove of hazel trees
    where the land turns above the draped slopes and the valley
with its one sunbeam and we exchange a few questions
    as though nothing were different but he has bulldozed the upland
pastures and shepherds' huts into piles of rubble
    and has his sheep fenced in everyone's meadows now
smell of box and damp leaves drifts from the woods where a blackbird
    is warning of nightfall and Baille has plans now to demolish
the ancient walls of the lane and level it wide
    so that trucks can go all the way down to where the lambs
with perhaps two weeks to live are waiting for him at the wire
    he hurried toward them as the sun sinks and the hour
turns chill as iron and in the oaks the first nightingales
    of the year kindle their unapproachable voices

OTHER TIME

There was a life several turns before this one
    and it woke to these seasons these same flowers this rain
these branches and roots of feeling that divide and divide again
    reaching into ruins into the treasures
and palaces of ruin and I knew the way then
    to a hundred ruins I could walk to in an hour
each with its own country and prospect its own birds
    and silence and in every roof part of the sky
that was the day I had come to be standing in
    which no one who had been born there had lived to see
whatever they may have watched from those hollow windows
    and coveted on those stairs that led up at last into trees
clear light went on staring out of the stone basins
    recalling clouds and I was in a future no one from there
could have conceived of or believed when they were sure
    that they would be there in it just as they were then
and not as strangers too long ago to be anyone

FRANÇOIS DE MAYNARD 1582–1646

When I cannot see my angel I would rather
    have been born blind and miserable I wrote at one time
then the season of flowers I said appeared to be
    painted black and it was impossible through those days
to imagine how I could have tarried so long
    on the earth while the syllables of thirty Aprils
had dripped like ice in the mountains and I had listened
    to the water as a song I might know and now
the autumn is almost done and the days arrive each one
    expecting less how long it is since I left
the court I loved once the passions there the skins of morning
    the colors of vain May and my hopes always for something
else that would be the same but more and never failing
    more praise more laurels more loves more bounty until I
could believe I was Ronsard and I wrote that I would have
    a monument as for a demigod whatever
that might be when I will be lucky to be buried
    as the poor are buried without noise and the faces covered
and be gone as the year goes out and be honored as a blank wall
    in a cold chapel of the church where I shivered as a child
beside my father the judge in his complete black those years when
    soldiers clattered and clanged through the streets horsemen clashed
under the windows and the nights rang with the screams
    of the wounded outside the walls while the farms burned
into dawns red with smoke and blood came spreading
    through the canals at the foot of those towers on the hill
that I would see again and again after every absence
    fingers of a hand rising out of the gray valley
in the distance and coming closer to become here as before
    where my mother wanted me where I married
where the banquets glittered along the river to my songs
    where my daughter died and how cold the house turned all at once
I have seen the waves of war come back and break over us here
    I have smelled rosemary and juniper burning in the plague
I have gone away and away I have held a post in Rome
    I have caught my death there I have flattered evil men
and gained nothing by it I have sat beside my wife
    when she could move no longer I sat here beside her
I watched the gold leaves of the poplars floating on the stream
    long ago the gold current of the river Pactolus

was compared to eternity but the poplar leaves have gone
 in the years when I rode to Aurillac I used to stop
at a place where the mountains appeared to open before me
 and turning I could still see all the way back to here
and both ways were my life which now I have slept through to wake
 in a dark house talking to the shadows about love

HÖLDERLIN AT THE RIVER

The ice again in my sleep it was following someone
    it thought was me in the dark and I recognized its white tongue
it held me in its freezing radiance until I
    was the only tree there and I broke and carried
my limbs down through dark rocks calling to the summer
    where are you where will you be how could I have missed you
gold skin the still pond shining under the eglantines
   warm peach resting in my palm at noon among flowers
all the way I was looking for you and I had nothing to say who I was
    until the last day of the world then far below I could see
the great valley as night fell the one ray withdrawing
    like the note of a horn and afterwards black wind took
all I knew but here is the foreign morning with its clouds
    sailing on water beyond the black trembling poplars
the sky breathless around its blinding fire and the white flocks
    in water meadows on the far shore are flowing past their
silent shepherds and now only once I hear the hammer
    ring on the anvil and in some place that I have not seen
a bird of ice is singing of its own country
    if any of this remains it will not be me

IN THE DOORWAY

From the stones of the door frame cold to the palm
 that breath of the dark sometimes from the chiselled
surfaces and at others from the places between them
 that chill and air without season that acrid haunting
that skunk ghost welcoming without welcome faithful without
 promise echo without echo it was there again
in the stones of the gate now in a new place but its own
 a place of leaving and returning that breath of belonging
and being distant of rain in box thickets
 part of it and of sheep in winter and the green stem
of the bee orchis in May that smell of abiding
 and not staying of a night breeze remembered only
in passing of fox shadow moss in autumn the bitter
 ivy the smell of the knife blade and of finding again
knowing no more but listening the smell of touching and going
 of what is gone the smell of touching and not being there

ONE OF THE LIVES

If I had not met the red-haired boy whose father
    had broken a leg parachuting into Provence
to join the resistance in the final stage of the war
    and so had been killed there as the Germans were moving north
out of Italy and if the friend who was with him
    as he was dying had not had an elder brother
who also died young quite differently in peacetime
    leaving two children one of them with bad health
who had been kept out of school for a whole year by an illness
    and if I had written anything else at the top
of the examination form where it said college
    of your choice or if the questions that day had been
put differently and if a young woman in Kittanning
    had not taught my father to drive at the age of twenty
so that he got the job with the pastor of the big church
    in Pittsburgh where my mother was working and if
my mother had not lost both parents when she was a child
    so that she had to go to her grandmother's in Pittsburgh
I would not have found myself on an iron cot
    with my head by the fireplace of a stone farmhouse
that had stood empty since some time before I was born
    I would not have travelled so far to lie shivering
with fever though I was wrapped in everything in the house
    nor have watched the unctuous doctor hold up his needle
at the window in the rain light of October
    I would not have seen through the cracked pane the darkening
valley with its river sliding past the amber mountains
    nor have wakened hearing plums fall in the small hour
thinking I knew where I was as I heard them fall

NIGHT SINGING

Long after Ovid's story of Philomela
    has gone out of fashion and after the testimonials
of Hafiz and Keats have been smothered in comment
    and droned dead in schools and after Eliot has gone home
from the Sacred Heart and Ransom has spat and consigned
    to human youth what he reduced to fairy numbers
after the name has become slightly embarrassing
    and dried skins have yielded their details and tapes have been
slowed and analyzed and there is nothing at all
    for me to say one nightingale is singing
nearby in the oaks where I can see nothing but darkness
    and can only listen and ride out on the long note's
invisible beam that wells up and bursts from its
    unknown star on on on never returning
never the same never caught while through the small leaves
    of May the starlight glitters from its own journeys
once in the ancestry of this song my mother visited here
    lightning struck the locomotive in the mountains
it had never happened before and there were so many
    things to tell that she had just seen and would never
have imagined now a field away I hear another
    voice beginning and on the slope there is a third
not echoing but varying after the lives
    after the goodbyes after the faces and the light
after the recognitions and the touching and tears
    those voices go on rising if I knew I would hear
in the last dark that singing I know how I would listen

UNTOUCHED

Even in dreams if I am there I keep trying
    to tell what is missing I have left friends in their days
I have left voices shimmering over the green field
    I have left the barns to the owls and the noon meadows
to the stealth of summer and again and again
    I have turned from it all and gone but it is not that
something was missing before that something was always
    not there I left the walls in their furs of snow
Esther calling the hens at dusk *petit petit*
    Viellescazes sucking the last joints of a story
Edouard bending into shadows to pick up walnuts
    before the leaves fell and I have left the weasel in the ivy
the lanes after midnight the clack of plates in the kitchen
    the feel of the door latch yielding it has hidden
in the presence of each of them whatever I missed
    I left the stream running under the mossy cliff

ROMANESQUE

Inside the light there was a stone and he knew it
    inside the stone there was a light and all day he kept
finding it the world in the light was stone
    built of stone held up by stone and in a stone house
you began you stood on a stone floor the fire played
    in its stone place and the sky in the window passed
between stones and outside the door your feet followed
    stones and when the fields were turned over in the light
they were made of stones the water came out of a stone
    some of the stones were faces with faces inside them
like every face and some of the stones were animals
    with animals inside them some of the stones were skies
with skies inside them and when he had worked long enough
    with stones touching them opening them looking inside
he saw that a day was a stone and the past was a stone
    with more darkness always inside it and the time to come
was a stone over a doorway and with his hand he formed
    the stone hand raised at the center and the stone face
under the stone sun and stone moon and he found the prophet
    who was stone prophesying stone he showed the stone limbs of
                                  childhood
and old age and the life between them holding up the whole
    stone of heaven and hell while the mother of us all
in her naked stone with the stone serpent circling
    her thigh went on smiling at something long after
he was forgotten she kept smiling at something he had known
    and at something he had never known at the time

DRY GROUND

Summer deepens and a root reaches for receding
　　water with a sense of waking long afterward
long after the main event whatever it was
　　has faded out like the sounds of a procession
like April like the age of dew like the beginning
　　now the dry grass dying keeps making the sounds of rain
to hollow air while the wheat whitens in the cracked fields
　　and they keep taking the cows farther up into the woods
to dwindling pools under the oaks and even there
　　the brown leaves are closing their thin hands and falling
and out on the naked barrens where the light shakes
　　in a fever without a surface and the parched shriek
of the cicadas climbs with the sun the bats
　　cling to themselves in crevices out of the light
and under stone roofs those who live watching the grapes
　　like foxes stare out over the plowed white stones
and see in all the hueless blaze of the day nothing
　　but rows of withered arms holding up the green grapes

BATTUES

Never more alien never born farther away
    never less acquiescent in all that on all sides
is taken for granted never hearing with such
    clarity the fatal intent of the voices
as when they ring the upland out of thickets
    along the edges of oak woods and beside hollows
still harboring sweet night and spring up from shadows
    in cleft rocks that gaze out over the naked
stony barrens those rough shouts suddenly struck from
    raw metals commanding the dogs whipping them on
echoing over the lit baying of the racing
    hounds those voices that have called to each other all
their lives growing up together with this pitch always
    in them they know it this fire shaking and beating
burning as one toward the careful cellars of badgers
    boars' coverts the tunnels of foxes the bursting owls
to the end of flight and the cornered eyes they go on
    I keep hearing them knowing them they are the cavalry
at Sand Creek they are Jackson's finest rooting out
    the infants of the Seminoles they are calling
names I know words we speak every day they are using
    language that we share which we say proves what we are

SNAKE

When it seemed to me that whatever was holding
    me there pretending to let me go but then bringing
me back each time as though I had never been gone
    and knowing me knowing me unseen among those rocks
when it seemed to me that whatever that might be
    had not changed for all my absence and still was not changing
once in the middle of the day late in that time
    I stood up from the writings unfinished on the table
in the echoless stone room looking over the valley
    I opened the door and on the stone doorsill
where every so often through the years I had come
    upon a snake lying out in the sunlight I found
the empty skin like smoke on the stone with the day
    still moving in it and when I touched it and lifted
all of it the whole thing seemed lighter than a single
    breath and then I was gone and that time had changed and when
I came again many years had passed and I saw
    one day along the doorsill outside that same room
a green snake lying in the sunlight watching me
    even from the eyes the skin loosens leaving the colors
that have passed through it and the colors shine after it has gone

VEHICLES

This is a place on the way after the distances
    can no longer be kept straight here in this dark corner
of the barn a mound of wheels has convened along
    ravelling courses to stop in a single moment
and lie down as still as the chariots of the Pharaohs
    some in pairs that rolled as one over the same roads
to the end and never touched each other until they
    arrived here some that broke by themselves and were left
until they could be repaired some that went only
    to occasions before my time and some that have spun
across other countries through uncounted summers
    now they go all the way back together the tall
cobweb-hung models of galaxies in their rings
    of rust leaning against the stone hail from René's
manure cart the year he wanted to store them here
    because there was nobody left who could make them like that
in case he should need them and there are the carriage wheels
    that Merot said would be worth a lot some day
and the rim of the spare from bald Bleret's green Samson
    that rose like Borobudur out of the high grass
behind the old house by the river where he stuffed
    mattresses in the morning sunlight and the hens
scavenged around his shoes in the days when the black
    top-hat sedan still towered outside Sandeau's cow barn
with velvet upholstery and sconces for flowers and room
    for two calves instead of the back seat when their time came

LATE

The old walls half fallen sink away under brambles
    and ivy and trail off into the oak woods that have been
coming back for them through all the lives whose daylight
    has vanished into the mosses there was a life once
in which I lived here part of a life believing
    in it partly as though it were the whole story
and so not a story at all and partly knowing
    that I clung to it only in passing as in
the words of a story and that partly I was still
    where I had come from and when I come back now later
and find it still here it seems to be a story
    I know but no longer believe and that is my place in it

SEASON

This hour along the valley this light at the end
    of summer lengthening as it begins to go
this whisper in the tawny grass this feather floating
    in the air this house of half a life or so
this blue door open to the lingering sun this stillness
    echoing from the rooms like an unfinished sound
this fraying of voices at the edge of the village
    beyond the dusty gardens this breath of knowing
without knowing anything this old branch from which
    years and faces go on falling this presence already
far away this restless alien in the cherished place
    this motion with no measure this moment peopled
with absences with everything that I remember here
    eyes the wheeze of the gate greetings birdsongs in winter
the heart dividing dividing and everything
    that has slipped my mind as I consider the shadow
all this has occurred to somebody else who has gone
    as I am told and indeed it has happened again
and again and I go on trying to understand
    how that could ever be and all I know of them
is what they felt in the light here in this late summer

EMERGENCE

From how many distances am I to arrive
    again and find I am standing on the bare outcrop
at the top of the ridge by the corner of the ancient wall
    with the sloe thickets the sheep tracks the gray ruins
oak woods abrupt hollows and the burials of the upland
    rolling away behind me farther than I can guess
and before me the path down through rocks and wild thyme
    into the village its tiled roofs washed out with sunlight
its trees glinting in the faded day and beyond them
    the valley blue and indelible as a vein
sometimes it is spring with the white blossoms opening
    their moments of light along the thin naked branches
sometimes snow has quilted the barns the houses the small fields
    the waves of moss on the walls but always it is autumn
with the rest inside it like skies seen in water
    and the summer days folded into the stones and I have come
not to live there once more nor to stay nor to touch
    nor to understand arriving from farther and farther
from the time of alien cities from the breathing
    of traffic from sleepless continents from the eye of water
from flying at altitudes at which nothing
    can survive and from the darkness and from afterward

THE SPEED OF LIGHT

So gradual in those summers was the going
     of the age it seemed that the long days setting out
when the stars faded over the mountains were not
     leaving us even as the birds woke in full song and the dew
glittered in the webs it appeared then that the clear morning
     opening into the sky was something of ours
to have and to keep and that the brightness we could not touch
     and the air we could not hold had come to be there all the time
for us and would never be gone and that the axle
     we did not hear was not turning when the ancient car
coughed in the roofer's barn and rolled out echoing
     first thing into the lane and the only tractor
in the village rumbled and went into its rusty
     mutterings before heading out of its lean-to
into the cow pats and the shadow of the lime tree
     we did not see that the swallows flashing and the sparks
of their cries were fast in the spokes of the hollow
     wheel that was turning and turning us taking us
all away as one with the tires of the baker's van
     where the wheels of bread were stacked like days in calendars
coming and going all at once we did not hear
     the rim of the hour in whatever we were saying
or touching all day we thought it was there and would stay
     it was only as the afternoon lengthened on its
dial and the shadows reached out farther and farther
     from everything that we began to listen for what
might be escaping us and we heard high voices ringing
     the village at sundown calling their animals home
and then the bats after dark and the silence on its road

OLD QUESTION

Can anyone tell me what became of the voices
    that rang here in the lane every morning at the beginning
of autumn those mornings those autumns if there were more
    than one and that was the way the autumn morning
was to begin then with a sound somewhere between bird echoes
    and brook water over pebbles coming closer
a flight of high bells the small girls from farther along
    the ridge walking to school some of them still with their hair
down to their waists or whatever happened to the voice
    of the head mason scolding later in the sunlight
at the house below the long field he kept rasping No
    No over the rasp of the shovels mixing wet mortar
I tell you No and they all kept right on at what they
    were doing knowing that it was simply the way
he always talked and the wall rose into the day
    and its own silence where it seemed to have been before
anyone could remember or in what country now
    is the sound of the gate that never went away

ONE TIME

When I was a child being taken home from the circus
    late at night in the rumble seat of the old car
in which I had never ridden and my head was afloat
    in the lap of a woman whom now I would think of
as young and who then was fragrant strange and as hard to believe
    as Christmas as she went on agreeing in a low voice
about how late it was and I kept watching her breath
    flying away into the cold night overhead
in which the naked stars were circling as we turned
    from the river and came up along the dark cliff
into our own echoes that wheeled us under the black
    leafless branches here it was already morning
and a figure whom I have known only bent with age
    was taking the cows out in his high youth onto
the untouched frost of the lanes and his burly son
    my neighbor was an infant and the woods furred the ridge
all the way down to the white fields with their pencilled walls
    the one cowbell rang cold and bright before him and crows
called across the blank pastures and early shadows

PEIRE VIDAL

I saw the wolf in winter watching on the raw hill
    I stood at night on top of the black tower and sang
I saw my mouth in spring float away on the river
    I was a child in rooms where the furs were climbing
and each was alone and they had no eyes no faces
    nothing inside them any more but the stories
but they never breathed as they waved in their dreams of grass
    and I sang the best songs that were sung in the world
as long as a song lasts and they came to me by themselves
    and I loved blades and boasting and shouting as I rode
as though I was the bright day flashing from everything
    I loved being with women and their breath and their skin
and the thought of them that carried me like a wind
    I uttered terrible things about other men
in a time when tongues were cut out to pay for a kiss
    but I set my sail for the island of Venus
and a niece of the Emperor in Constantinople
    and I could have become the Emperor myself
I won and I won and all the women in the world
    were in love with me and they wanted what I wanted
so I thought and every one of them deceived me
    I was the greatest fool in the world I was the world's fool
I have been forgiven and have come home as I dreamed
    and seen them all dancing and singing as the ship came in
and I have watched friends die and have worn black and cut off
    the tails and ears of all my horses in mourning
and have shaved my head and the heads of my followers
    I have been a poor man living in a rich man's house
and I have gone back to the mountains and for one woman
    I have worn the fur of a wolf and the shepherds' dogs
have run me to earth and I have been left for dead
    and have come back hearing them laughing and the furs
were hanging in the same places and I have seen
    what is not there I have sung its song I have breathed
its day and it was nothing to you where were you

THE VIEW

No wonder there are those lights of suspicion moving
    endlessly over memory and its faces
over the way of memory itself the way
    of remembering which is the way of forgetting
the way of horizons the way beyond reach the way
    of another which appears at times to be the only way
when not one thing not one moment with its heavenly
    bodies flying through unrepeated places not one
sound or shining is what it was the one time before
    it was remembered when I was in the midst of it
looking out thinking about something far from there
    bodies and death and taxes and what I did not want
and have forgotten while Lande was plowing the length
    of the field under the walnut trees in September
for the last time going on talking to the cows
    tapping lightly on their yoke with the slender stick
that he had cut in the hazel grove one year when he
    was young I watched the cows follow him out of the field
and the shadows filled it and the small lights appeared in the valley
    each of them coming from what was already gone

OLD WALLS

When the year has turned on its mountain as the summer
    stars begin to grow faint and the wren wakes into
singing I am waiting among the loosening stones
    of the enclosure beyond the lower door of the far barn
the green stitchwort shines in the new light as though it were
    still spring and no footprint leads through it any longer
the one apple tree has not grown much in its corner
    the ivy has taken over the east wall toward the oak woods
and crept into the bird cherry here I listened
    to the clack of the old man's hoe hilling the potatoes
in his dry field below the ash trees and here I looked up
    into the quince flowers opening above the wall
and I wanted to be far away like the surface
    of a river I knew and here I watched the autumn light
and thought this was where I might choose to be buried
    here I struggled in the web and went on weaving it
with every turn and here I went on yielding
    too much credit to an alien claim and here I came
to myself in a winter fog with ice on the stones
    and I went out through the gap in the wall and it was done
and here I thought I saw myself as I had once been
    and I was certain that I was free of an old chain

THE FURROW

Did I think it would abide as it was forever
    all that time ago the turned earth in the old garden
where I stood in spring remembering spring in another place
    that had ceased to exist and the dug roots kept giving up
their black tokens their coins and bone buttons and shoe nails
    made by hands and bits of plates as the thin clouds
of that season slipped past gray branches on which the early
    white petals were catching their light and I thought I knew
something of age then my own age which had conveyed me
    to there and the ages of the trees and the walls and houses
from before my coming and the age of the new seeds as I
    set each one in the ground to begin to remember
what to become and the order in which to return
    and even the other age into which I was passing
all the time while I was thinking of something different

THE TIME BEFORE

Out on the upland before I was there to see
    they were walking over the bare stone carrying
their shoes because it was going to be a long way
    their day was ringing the barrens in a loud wind
and they were taking their seasons with them as animals
    through the beating light urging on the sheep of autumn
the pigs of winter the lambs of spring the cows of summer
    all heading the same way along the rough walls of the lanes
so old that they had no beginnings and no memory
    their voices and the sounds of their feet flew up from them like
flocks of finches and blew away with all the names that they
    used for themselves and were continually saying
and all the words that were what they had then and were what they
    were saying to each other as they went along and as they
greeted each other when they met where the lanes came
    together and when they told where they were going

PORTRAIT

One ninth of March when for reasons that we can only
    suppose Monseigneur who bore the name of a saint
gone into legend had wished to be rendered immortal
    in tapestry and he had for his agent in this
affair none other than the priest who was
    precentor and canon at the cathedral named for
the same saint the said priest signing for him on the one hand
    and Adrian a merchant from Brabant on the other
having made certain pacts and agreements touching upon
    the design and depicting of the same Monseigneur
to be portrayed with his story in lengths of tapestry
    of certain form and style determined by those same
the said tapestry to be brought by said Adrian
    to the city of Bordeaux and left in the house
of honest Yzabeau Bertault widow for her
    to send it on to the said priest after making
payment of certain moneys and on this same day
    said delivery having been made and said payment
given before two further agents of Monseigneur
    because they themselves were not qualified to say
whether said tapestry made up of eight lengths six long
    two short was of the same worth and value that the same
Adrian claimed and was receiving namely two hundred
    forty livres ten sous two other merchants experts
of that city were present to bear witness to its worth
    there is no tapestry only the signatures

POSSESSIONS

Such vast estates such riches beyond estimation
>of course they all came out of the ground at some time
out of dark places before the records were awake
>they were held by hands that went out like a succession of flames
as the land itself was held until it named its
>possessors who described and enumerated it
in front of magistrates dividing the huge topography
>multiplying the name extending the chateau
house gardens fields woods pastures those facing
>the hill of Argentat with also the road leading
through them and the land called Murat and the fields and woods
>of the hill of Courtis and other designated
dependencies chapel stables dovecote additional
>lands south of the lane to which others were added by
marriage by death by purchase by reparation
>complicating the names of the legitimate offspring
lengthening the testaments that were meant to leave nothing out
>furnishings plates linens each mirror and its frame
the barrels and oxen and horses and sows and sheep
>the curtained beds the contents of the several kitchens
besides all such personal belongings as money
>and jewels listed apart which were considerable
by the time Madame la Vicomtesse who was heir to it all
>found it poor in variety and after her marriage
was often away visiting family and so on
>leaving the chateau in the keeping of her
father-in-law who was almost totally deaf
>so it happened that one night during a violent
thunderstorm the son of a laborer managed
>to climb through an upper window and into Madame's
bedroom where with the point of a plowshare he opened
>her jewel case and removed everything in it
and two nights later the gold crown studded with precious
>stones that was a gift of His Holiness Pius the Ninth
also was missing it was these absences
>that were commemorated at the next family wedding
at which the Vicomtesse wore at her neck and wrists
>pink ribbons in place of the jewels that had been hers
it was for the ribbons that she was remembered

LEGACIES

When he was beginning perhaps to feel his age
    Louis the carpenter one sunny day in spring
took me and his elder son who was then a thin
    young man to look at his walnut trees still without
leaves on their new branches that waved like wands above the clouds
    of sloe bushes in full flower along the hedges
up on the land plowed in the autumn on the windswept
    ridge those fields that had come to him from his grandmother
who had lived beside them once in the hamlet
    under the old lime trees where only the barns by the time
I saw it were inhabited it was just sheep now he told me
    we could hear them calling in the pastures beyond the roofs
and he said that when those walnut trees were planted
    a few years back when his son was a child they had dug
down to the limestone and had tipped into each hole
    half a cart load of wool waste left over from the carding machine
there were finches blowing across the blue sky behind
    the bare limbs as he talked and he touched the young trees
with their grafting scars still plain on the bark and their branches
    formed of wool that had grown through a single summer
and come back to winter barns carrying the day's weather

THE RED

It was summer a bright day in summer and the path kept
    narrowing as it led in under the oaks
which grew larger than those I was used to in that country
    darker and mossed like keepers it seemed to me
of an age earlier than anything I could know
    underfoot the ground became damp and water appeared
in long scarves on the trail between overhanging
    ferns and bushes and reflected the sky through the leaves
the birds were silent at that hour and I went on
    through the cool air listening and came to a corner
of ruined wall where the way emerged into
    a bare place in the woods with paths coming together
the remains of walls going on under trees and the roofless
    shoulders of stone buildings standing hunched among heavy
boughs all in shade the mud tracks of animals led
    past a tall stone in the center darker than the stone
of that country and with polished faces and red
    lines across them which when I came close I saw
were names cut deep into the stone and beside each one
    a birth date with each letter and numeral painted
that fresh crimson I read without counting to the foot
    of one side and the date of death and the account
of how it had come to them one day in summer when they
    were brought out of those buildings where they had lived
old people most of them as the dates indicated
    men and women and with them children they had been
ordered in German to that spot where they were
    shot then the Germans set fire to the buildings
with the animals inside and when they had finished
    they went off down the lane and the fires burned on
and the smoke filled the summer twilight and then the warm night

COMPLETION

Seen from afterward the time appears to have been
    all of a piece which of course it was but how seldom
it seemed that way when it was still happening and was
    the air through which I saw it as I went on thinking
of somewhere else in some other time whether gone
    or never to arrive and so it was divided
however long I was living it and I was where
    it kept coming together and where it kept moving apart
while home was a knowledge that did not suit every occasion
    but remained familiar and foreign as the untitled days
and what I knew better than to expect followed me
    into the garden and I would stand with friends among
the summer oaks and be a city in a different
    age and the dread news arrived on the morning when the plum trees
opened into silent flower and I could not let go
    of what I longed to be gone from and it would be that way
without end I thought unfinished and divided
    by nature and then a voice would call from the field
in the evening or the fox would bark in the cold night
    and that instant with each of its stars just where it was
in its unreturning course would appear even then
    entire and itself the way it all looks from afterward

PASSING

One dark afternoon in the middle of the century
    I came over a low rise into the light rain
that was drifting in veils out over the exposed barrens
    long long after the oak forests had been forgotten
long after the wandering bands and the last lines
    of horsemen carrying the raised moments of kings
a few surviving sparrows flew up ahead of me
    from gray splinters of grass hidden under the bitter
thymes and across the stony plain a flurry of sheep
    was inching like a shadow they had the rain behind them
they were stopping to nose the scattered tufts while two silent
    dogs kept moving them on and two boys with blankets
on their shoulders would bend one at a time to pick up
    a stone and throw it to show the dogs where to close in
on the straggling flock the far side of it already
    swallowed up in the mist and I stood watching
as they went picking up stones and throwing them farther
    and the dogs racing to where the stones fell the sheep starting up
running a few steps and stopping again all of them
    flowing together like one cloud tearing and gathering
I stood there as they edged on and I wanted to call
    to them as they were going I stood still wanting
to call out something at least before they had disappeared

SUBSTANCE

I could see that there was a kind of distance lighted
    behind the face of that time in its very days
as they appeared to me but I could not think of any
    words that spoke of it truly nor point to anything
except what was there at the moment it was beginning
    to be gone and certainly it could not have been proven
nor held however I might reach toward it touching
    the warm lichens the features of the stones the skin
of the river and I could tell then that it was
    the animals themselves that were the weight and place
of the hour as it happened and that the mass of the cow's neck
    the flash of the swallow the trout's flutter were
where it was coming to pass they were bearing the sense of it
    without questions through the speechless cloud of light

THE SHORTEST NIGHT

All of us must have been asleep when it happened
    after the long day of summer and that steady
clarity without shadows that stayed on around us
    and appeared not to change or to fade when the sun
had gone and the red had drained from the sky and the single
    moment of chill had passed scarcely noticed across
the mown fields and the mauve valley where the colors were stopped
    and after the hush through which the ends of voices
made their way from their distances when the swallows
    had settled for the night and the notes of the cuckoo
echoed along the slope and the milking was finished
    and the calves and dogs were closed in the breath of the barns
and we had sat talking almost in whispers long past
    most bedtimes in the village and yet lights were not lit
we talked remembering how far each of us had come
    to be there as the trembling bats emerged from
the small veins in the wall above us and sailed out
    calling and we meant to stay up and see the night
at the moment when it turned with the calves all asleep
    by then and the dogs curled beside them and Edouard
and Esther both older than the century sleeping
    in another age and the children still sleeping
in the same bed and the hens down tight on their perches
    the stones sleeping in the garden walls and the leaves
sleeping in the sky where there was still light with the owls
    slipping by like shadows and the moles listening
the foxes listening the ears the feet some time there
    we must have forgotten what we had meant to stay
awake for and it all turned away when we were not
    looking I thought I had flown over the edge
of the world I could call to and that I was still flying
    and had to wake to learn whether the wings were real

A TASTE

When the first summer there was ending more than half
    my life ago Mentières with his strawberry nose
and features to match and his eyes stitched down inside them
    in the shade of his black-vizored cap which proclaimed
to the world that he had taken his retirement
    not from the land but from the railroad Mentières with his
leer and his vest stretched over his large protuberance
    and his walk like a barrel neither full nor empty
he whom nobody trusted thereabouts laying their
    fingers beside their noses Mentières from elsewhere
the custodian of keys who had no land of his own
    so had been using the garden to grow his potatoes in
and had been picking up the plums from under the trees
    to make his own plum as he put it meaning of course
clear alcohol the water of life but it was
    too hard for him to bend any more in his striped
trousers to hoe the furrows and grope for the plums
    and he would not be doing it another year
so he brought back the big keys and with them a couple of
    old corked bottles from the year before and another
already opened for tasting the pure stuff the essence
    of plum to breathe it down your nose
and out like watching your breath on a winter day
    that was what kept them warm in the trenches he told me
a drop of that in your coffee he said holding up
    a thick finger and when his wife fell sick everyone
said they were sorry for her and when she died they said
    they were sorry for the daughter who never married
and looked after him he sat on the front step watching
    the road and waving to anyone but when he was gone
nobody seemed to notice the cork is beginning
    to crumble but the taste is the same as it was
the pure plum of the year before that has no color

UPLAND HOUSE

The door was not even locked and all through the day
    light came in between the boards as it had always done
through each of the lives there the one life of sunlight slipping
    so slowly that it would have appeared to be
not moving if anyone had been there to notice
    but they were all gone by then while it went on tracing the way
by heart over the cupped floorboards the foot of the dark bed
    in the corner the end of the table covered
with its crocheted cloth once white and the dishes yet on it
    candlestick bottles stain under one bulge in the black
ceiling the ranges of cobwebs roots of brambles
    fingering the fireplace the line continued across them
in silence not taking anything with it as
    it travelled through its own transparent element
I watched it move and everything I remembered
    had happened in a country with a different language
and when I remembered that house I would not be the same

BODIES OF WATER

In the long stone basin under the apple tree
      at the end of one spring in the garden I saw the faces
of all the masons who had built there on the edge
      of the rock overlooking the valley their reflections
smiled out from the still surface into the speechless
      daylight each of them for a moment the only one
with all the others lined up in them like stairs I could not
      see whether they led up or down then a wind rustled
across the garden waking it to the time it was then
      turning to summer in one of whose days I came
to the old trees off by themselves on the bleached hill
      cool darkness under them suddenly and the largest
stood at the end of a green where a fountain
      chattered on into a stone basin and on each side
among the shadow were stone walls and the shuttered ruins
      of a village with one stone arch leading into a courtyard
before a tall house and tower and a barn beyond them
      by the open house door an old man was sitting
who told me that it was the place where he had lived
      all his life and he said he would soon be ninety
now he slept up on the hill with his great-grandchildren
      who would sell whatever they could but he assured me
he would sell nothing in his lifetime this was where he came
      every day and sat by the door under the lime tree
and now look he said standing and walking slowly
      past the barn and pointing to five slender walnut trees
fifteen years from the seed he said and I grafted them
      last year myself and every one of them took
he said these give me something to look forward to

AFTER FIRES

In the time when witches were still burning and
    the word of the king meant so little in the mountains
that tribunals were dispatched into the outlying
    darkness with power to administer the law
on the spot a woman was brought in one day accused
    of burning down two or three houses and perhaps more
for the courtiers were given to understand
    that this was customary in the region when someone
had been displeased and when the snow was upon the mountain
    then they set their fires but the setting was hard to prove
for the fires were plotted in secret and set at night
    and when it was said that she had been seen leaving
her house after dark carrying fire and later
    that night a house had burned she denied any part in it
and the witness was muddled and useless and although
    it was plain that this was a woman of unsavory
conduct she having produced several children without
    being married which she said was the men's doing
when she was condemned to the question a matter
    in that place of nothing more than a violent
stretching she bore it with firmness and confessed nothing
    saying only that the judge hoped for a reason
for hanging her and so at last she was branded
    with the lily and banished to burn some said other houses
and beget other offspring I thought of her long after
    she had gone like smoke and after those courts were dust
and after the time when everyone stopped in the middle
    of the noon meal in a moment of autumn sunlight
and suddenly we were running up the white road
    toward the column of dark smoke rising out of itself
swelling and unfurling into the blue sky over
    the ridge we were halfway there before the first bells
rang behind us too late too late and when we came in sight
    the neighbors had carried out the old woman and left her
on a mattress on the ground she was not even watching
    the neighbors throwing their buckets of water and
her son dragging out one smoking thing after another
    none of them what he wanted he had not been there
when it began and nobody knew how it started
    so everyone informed everyone as the fire truck

finally got there and the hoses began unrolling
    then the firemen and the son were sorting through the hissing
remnants and fallen stones trying to find a box
    as everyone told everyone and the old woman
said yes there was the box they should look for the box
    it was all in the box the papers and the money and they
peered under the rubble with the smoke still
    threading upward from the charred ends of rafters
she said the box was made of iron it was under the stairs
    which were no longer there they found it at last the iron
too hot to touch and they wet it down and took it
    to the old woman who nodded but then they were
some time getting it open since the key was lost and the hoses
    went on playing the rest of the tank of water
onto the ruins through the glass dome of the afternoon
    and the ring of the curious was hushed around the mattress
when the son pried the lid off letting us all see
    that there was nothing inside but a small drift of black snow

THREAD

One morning a single bead turns up in the garden
    some kind of glass filled now with dark soil where the silk went
when they were all here together picking up the light
    it seemed that they had always been the age they were then
and that they would never be different even Viellescazes
    transparent as a doorway who sat through his late days
on the wall in the shade by the road where stories
    came back to him from so long before that they sounded
like a former life Esther who lulled her complaining knees
    hunched on the bench beside a few embers and mumbled
about dogs Edouard at eighty sickling the new grass
    under the plum trees in the cool summer mornings
one by one they dropped away and this winter Richard
    the mason with the long face white as a baker's
went and Berg who was stricken driving his tractor
    and survived to kneel for hours by his peonies
quiet people never divulging much and this spring
    Adrienne died in the home where she had taken
to going for the cold months she had not thought she would
    last so long after Jean her husband the cloud-voiced
roofer was buried but after a while she went on
    riding her bicycle slowly and smiling like a passing queen
and she was still in demand when they killed a pig anywhere
    famous as she had become for the way she made sausage
they say nobody ever managed to learn how she did it

THE CISTERNS

At intervals across the crumpled barrens
    where brambles and sloes are leading back the shy oaks
to touch the fallen roofs the leaves brush flat stones under which
    in single notes a covered music is staring
upward into darkness and listening for the rest of it
    after a long time lying in the deep stone without
moving and without breath and without forgetting
    in all that unmeasured silence the least of the sounds
remembered by water since the beginning
    whir of being carried in clouds sigh of falling
chatter of stream thunders crashes the rush of echoes
    and the ringing of drops falling from stones in the dark
moment by moment and the echoes of voices
    of cows calling and of the whispers of straw and of the cries
of each throat sounding over the one still continuo
    of the water and the echoes sinking in their turns
into the memory of the water the tones
    one here one there of an art no longer practised

ANCESTRAL VOICES

In the old dark the late dark the still deep shadow
    that had travelled silently along itself all night
while the small stars of spring were yet to be seen and the few
    lamps burned by themselves with no expectations
far down through the valley then suddenly the voice
    of the blackbird came believing in the habit
of the light until the torn shadows of the ridges
    that had gone out one behind the other into the darkness
began appearing again still asleep surfacing in their
    dream and the stars all at once were gone and instead the song
of the blackbird flashed through the unlit boughs and far
    out in the oaks a nightingale went on echoing
itself drawing out its own invisible starlight
    these voices were lifted here long before the first
of our kind had come to be able to listen
    and with the faint light in the dew of the infant
leaves goldfinches flew out from their nests in the brambles
    they had chosen their colors for the day and they sang
of themselves which was what they had wakened to remember

OLD SOUND

The walls of the house are old as I think of them
    they have always been old as long as I have known
their broken limestone the colors of dry grass patched
    with faded mortar containing the rusted earth
of the place itself from which the stones too had been
    taken up and set in the light of days that no one
has known anything about for generations
    many lives had begun and ended inside there
and had passed over the stone doorsill and looked from the windows
    to see faces arriving under trees that are not
there any more with the sky white behind them and doorways
    had been sealed up inside the squared stones of their frames
and fires that left the stones of one corner red
    and cracked had gone cold even in their legends
the house had come more than once to an end and had stood
    empty for half a lifetime and been abandoned
by the time I saw the roof half shrouded in brambles
    and picked my way to peer through the hole in the crumbling
wall at the rubble on the floor and ivy swaying
    in the small north window across the room now the house
is another age in my mind it is old to me
    in ways I thought I knew but they go on changing
now its age is made of almost no time a sound
    that you have to get far away from before you hear it

GREEN FIELDS

By this part of the century few are left who believe
    in the animals for they are not there in the carved parts
of them served on plates and the pleas from the slatted trucks
    are sounds of shadows that possess no future
there is still game for the pleasure of killing
    and there are pets for the children but the lives that followed
courses of their own other than ours and older
    have been migrating before us some are already
far on the way and yet Peter with his gaunt cheeks
    and point of white beard the face of an aged Lawrence
Peter who had lived on from another time and country
    and who had seen so many things set out and vanish
still believed in heaven and said he had never once
    doubted it since his childhood on the farm in the days
of the horses he had not doubted it in the worst
    times of the Great War and afterward and he had come
to what he took to be a kind of earthly
    model of it as he wandered south in his sixties
by that time speaking the language well enough
    for them to make him out he took the smallest roads
into a world he thought was a thing of the past
    the wild flowers he scarcely remembered the neighbors
working together scything the morning meadows
    turning the hay before the noon meal bringing it in
by milking time husbandry and abundance
    all the virtues he admired and their reward bounteous
in the eyes of a foreigner and there he remained
    for the rest of his days seeing what he wanted to see
until the winter when he could no longer fork
    the earth in his garden and then he gave away
his house land everything and committed himself
    to a home to die in an old chateau where he lingered
for some time surrounded by those who had lost
    the use of body or mind and as he lay there he told me
that the wall by his bed opened almost every day
    and he saw what was really there and it was eternal life
as he recognized at once when he saw the gardens
    he had planted and the green field where he had been
a child and his mother was standing there then the wall would close
    and around him again were the last days of the world

DISTANT MORNING

We were a time of our own the redstart reappeared
    on the handle of the fork left alone for that moment
upright in the damp earth the shriek of the black kite
    floated high over the river as the day warmed
the weasel slipped like a trick of light through the ivy
    there was one wryneck pretending to be a shadow
on the trunk of a dead plum tree while the far figures
    of daylight crossed the dark crystal of its eye
the tawny owl clenched itself in the oak hearing the paper
    trumpet and rapid knocking that told where the nuthatch
prospected and the gray adder gathered itself
    on its gray stone with the ringing of a cricket suspended
around it the nightwalkers slept curled in their houses
    the hedgehogs in the deep brush the badgers and foxes
in their home ground the bats high under the eaves
    none of it could be held or denied or summoned back
none of it would be given its meaning later

VIXEN

Comet of stillness princess of what is over
    high note held without trembling without voice without sound
aura of complete darkness keeper of the kept secrets
    of the destroyed stories the escaped dreams the sentences
never caught in words warden of where the river went
    touch of its surface sibyl of the extinguished
window onto the hidden place and the other time
    at the foot of the wall by the road patient without waiting
in the full moonlight of autumn at the hour when I was born
    you no longer go out like a flame at the sight of me
you are still warmer than the moonlight gleaming on you
    even now you are unharmed even now perfect
as you have always been now when your light paws are running
    on the breathless night on the bridge with one end I remember you
when I have heard you the soles of my feet have made answer
    when I have seen you I have waked and slipped from the calendars
from the creeds of difference and the contradictions
    that were my life and all the crumbling fabrications
as long as it lasted until something that we were
    had ended when you are no longer anything
let me catch sight of you again going over the wall
    and before the garden is extinct and the woods are figures
guttering on a screen let my words find their own
    places in the silence after the animals

A GIVEN DAY

When I wake I find it is late in the autumn
    the hard rain has passed and the sunlight has not yet reached
the tips of the dark leaves that are their own shadows still
    and I am home it is coming back to me I am
remembering the gradual sweetness of morning
    the clear spring of being here as it rises one by one
in silence and without a pause and is the only one
    then one at a time I remember without understanding
some that have gone and arise only not to be here
    an afternoon walking on a bridge thinking of a friend
when she was still alive while a door from a building
    being demolished sailed down through the passing city
my mother half my age at a window long since removed
    friends in the same rooms and the words dreaming between us
the eyes of animals upon me they are all here
    in the clearness of the morning in the first light
that remembers its way now to the flowers of winter

W. S. Merwin was born in New York City in 1927 and grew up in Union City, New Jersey, and in Scranton, Pennsylvania. From 1949 to 1951 he worked as a tutor in France, Portugal, and Majorca. After that, for several years he made the greater part of his living by translating from French, Spanish, Latin, and Portuguese. In addition to poetry, he has written articles, chiefly for *The Nation*, and radio scripts for the BBC. He has lived in Spain, England, France, Mexico, and Hawaii, as well as New York City. His books of poetry are *A Mask for Janus* (1952), *The Dancing Bears* (1954), *Green with Beasts* (1956), *The Drunk in the Furnace* (1960), *The Moving Target* (1963), *The Lice* (1967), *The Carrier of Ladders* (1970), for which he was awarded the Pulitzer Prize, *Writings to an Unfinished Accompaniment* (1973), *The Compass Flower* (1977), *Opening the Hand* (1983), and *The Rain in the Trees* (1988). His translations include *The Poem of the Cid* (1959), *Spanish Ballads* (1961), *The Satires of Persius* (1960), *Lazarillo de Tormes* (1962), *The Song of Roland* (1963), *Selected Translations 1948–1968* (1968), for which he won the PEN Translation Prize for 1968, *Transparence of the World*, a translation of his selection of poems by Jean Follain (1969), *Osip Mandelstam, Selected Poems* (with Clarence Brown) (1974), *Selected Translations 1968–1978, Iphigeneia at Aulis* of Euripides, with George Dimock, Jr. (1978), *Vertical Poetry*, a selection of poems by Roberto Juarroz (1988) and *Sun at Midnight*, a selection of poems by Musō Soseki, translated with Sōiku Shigematsu (1989). He has also published four books of prose, *The Miner's Pale Children* (1970), *Houses and Travellers* (1977), *Unframed Originals* (1982), and *The Lost Upland* (1992). He has been a recipient of several fellowships, including Rockefeller, Guggenheim, Rabinowitz, NEA, Chapelbrook grants, and awards including the Bollingen, the Harriet Monroe, Shelley, Maurice English, Oscar Williams and Gene Derwood, and Aiken-Taylor prizes for poetry. In 1974 he was awarded the Fellowship of the Academy of American Poets. In 1987 he received the Governor's Award for Literature of the state of Hawaii. Since then he has been the recipient of The Tanning Prize for mastery in the art of poetry, and the Lenore Marshall Poetry Prize for *Travels* (1993). He has also been the recipient (1994) of a Lila Wallace-Reader's Digest Writers' Award.

A NOTE ON THE TYPE

This book was set on the Linotype in Janson, a recutting made direct from type cast from matrices long thought to have been made by the Dutchman Anton Janson, who was a practicing type founder in Leipzig during the years 1668–1687. However, it has been conclusively demonstrated that these types are actually the work of Nicholas Kis (1650–1702), a Hungarian, who most probably learned his trade from the master Dutch type founder Dirk Voskens. The type is an excellent example of the influential and sturdy Dutch types that prevailed in England up to the time William Caslon (1692–1766) developed his own incomparable designs from them.

Typesetting by Heritage Printers, Inc., Charlotte, North Carolina
Printed and bound by Quebecor Printing, Kingsport, Tennessee
Designed by Harry Ford